Are You Still Fighting With Your Y.E.S.

(Your Expected Submission)

Thomas C. Marbury

Are You Still Fighting With Your Y.E.S. (Your Expected Submission)

Copyright © 2014 by Thomas C. Marbury

All rights reserved. No part of this book may be reproduced or transmitted in any form– electronic, mechanical, photographic (photocopying), recording, or otherwise – or by any means without written permission from the author.

Unless otherwise noted, all Scripture quotations are from the New King James Version of the Bible Copyright © 1982 by Thomas Nelson, Inc. Used by permission. All rights reserved.
http://www.nelsonbibles.com/

Scripture quotations marked "AMP" are taken from the Amplified® Bible, Copyright © 1954, 1958, 1962, 1964, 1965, 1987 by The Lockman Foundation. Used by permission. www.Lockman.org

Scripture quotations marked (NIV) are taken from the Holy Bible, New International Version®, NIV®.
Copyright © 1973, 1978, 1984 by Biblica, Inc.™
Used by permission of Zondervan. All rights reserved worldwide.
http://www.zondervan.com

Scripture quotations marked "MSG" or "The Message" are taken from The Message. Copyright 1993, 1994, 1995, 1996, 2000, 2001, 2002. Used by permission of NavPress Publishing Group.
http://www.navpress.com/

ISBN 978-0-9905163-0-9 (trade paper
ISBN 978-0-9905163-1-6 (e-book)
Published in United States of America by Faith Walk Publishing
Learn More Info At:
www.thomascmarbury.com
www.faithwalkpublishing.com

Dedication

First and foremost, I thank God for my calling and sending. I thank all those who have prayed and supported the ministry work. Specifically, I thank my apostle/dad H. Daniel Wilson for pouring into me. I thank my wife Tamara for your continuous prayers & support; my mom (mother Scott) for your encouragement; and a special thanks to my daughter Danica whom God used to help bring this project to pass.

Table of Contents

Copyright ii

Dedication iii

Introduction 1

Section I Disobedient Servant 3

    When you say "Yes!" 3

    God's Correction for another Direction 4

    Whether obedient or disobedient, God is still working 5

    God will use sinners to spiritually wake you up 6

Section II Servant Exposed 8

    Your calling is always BIGGER than you think 8

    Where you've been determines where you are going 9

    Identifying the SOURCE and the SOURCE 11

    Getting rid of your no for YES 11

Section III The Belly Of Preparation 14

    ISOLATION 14

    SEPARATION 15

    SANCTIFICATION 16

Section IV Servant Reflection and Freedom 19

    The servant acknowledges God's Sovereignty 19

    The servant submits to God's Sovereignty 22

Section V The Lord Speaks/The Servant Hears 25
    When God Speaks 25
    The role of the enemy 26
    Ears to Hear 27
    The People are Waiting 27
    God is Not Through With You Yet 29
Conclusion 33
About The Author 35

Introduction

"Now the word of the LORD came to Jonah the son of Amittai, saying, 'Arise, go to Nineveh, that great city, and cry out against it; for their wickedness has come up before Me'" (Jonah 1:1, 2, NKJV).

What does it mean "Fighting with Your Yes?" There is a "Yes" that says, Lord I accept what you've done for me through the cross and your blood which led me to salvation (Rom. 10:9, 10). Then, there is another "Yes" that says, Lord, I am willing to do the work that you've called me to do (MY ASSIGNMENT). Just as it was with the prophet Jonah, this book is for those who struggle with the latter.

Besides Jonah, there were several other biblical characters that were fighting with their YES: Moses, Gideon, Isaiah, and Jeremiah, just to name a few. But the difference is that they were dealing with their own insecurities about themselves. In the case of Jonah, he was already doing the work and walking in his calling (2 Kg. 14:25); but it was his attitude about where and who God wanted him to minister to.

One thing that we must all learn and understand is that many times when FIGHTING WITH YOUR YES, it is actually fighting with your FLESH!

(5) "For those who live according to the flesh set their minds on the things of the flesh, but those who live according to the Spirit, the things of the Spirit. (8) So then, those who are in the flesh cannot please God" (Romans 8:5, 8).

In this book there are several aspects of Jonah's life and calling that we want to examine that were not pleasing to God; and at the end I pray that we will all come to the same conclusion based on the scripture: (28) "And we know that all things work together for good to those who love God, to those who are the called according to His purpose. (29) For whom He foreknew, He also predestined to be conformed to the image of His Son... (30) Moreover whom He predestined, these He also called; whom He called, these He also justified; and whom He justified, these He also glorified" (Romans 8:28-30).

Lord Jesus, I thank you for every Y.E.S. (Your Expected Submission) that comes through this book! In your name... Amen!

Section I Disobedient Servant

"Arise, go to Nineveh, that great city, and cry out against it: for their wickedness has come up before Me" **(Jonah 1:2).**

When you say "Yes!"

When you say "Yes" to the call of God on your life you don't have the option to decide who you should minister to. The Lord calls us not just to salvation, but after that we are to be a light to those who don't know Him and are just as we were. This is why when Jesus went to Levi's house for a feast, and the religious leaders began to complain and talk against Jesus and His disciples about whom they chose to be around (tax collectors & sinners), Jesus said, *"Those who are well have no need of a physician, but those who are sick. (32) I have not come to call the righteous, but sinners to repentance"* (Luke 5:31, 32). The Lord's concern is always for the lost and He will give all a chance to come to repentance. The key is that He wants to use US to do it!

Nineveh was a place that Jonah would not have gone on his own because Nineveh was an enemy to Israel (Isaiah 37:8-38). How many of us who are saved and filled with the Spirit of God (Acts 1:8), want to determine who we minister to? Jesus even said, *(43) "You have heard that it was said, 'You shall love your neighbor and hate your enemy.' (44) But I say to you, love your enemies, bless those who curse you, do good to those who hate you, and pray for those who spitefully use you and persecute you, (45) that you may be sons of your Father in heaven; for He makes His sun rise on the evil and on the good, and sends rain on the just and on the unjust"* (Matthew 5:43-45).

Many times when God is sending you it is a time of dealing with your carnal attitude (the flesh). For your ATTITUDE determines your ALTITUDE! When your attitude is not right before God, He has to put you in a position that it will manifest. When the Lord said *"Arise"* there was a spiritual stirring up; but when He said, *"go to Nineveh,"* the flesh took over.

God's Correction for another Direction

"But Jonah arose to flee to Tarshish from the presence of the LORD. He went down to Joppa, and found a ship

going to Tarshish; so he paid the fare, and went down into it, to go with them to Tarshish from the presence of the LORD" (Jonah 1:3).

Because Jonah was unwilling to do what the Lord called him to do, he went in a totally opposite direction. The text says he went down to Joppa and paid his fare and then went DOWN into the ship. Verse 5 says, *"Jonah had gone down into the lowest parts of the ship."* His disobedience carried him as low as he could go. Disobedience will always take you down the wrong path and ultimately it will cost you something if not everything! This was the beginning of God's judgment towards His prophet.

"But the LORD sent out a great wind on the sea, and there was a mighty tempest on the sea, so that the ship was about to be broken" (Jonah 1:4).

Sin doesn't just affect the sinner, it affects ALL. It affects the atmosphere of humanity and nature.

Whether obedient or disobedient, God is still working

"Then the mariners were afraid; and every man cried out to his god, and threw the cargo that was in the ship into the sea, to lighten the load. But Jonah had gone down

into the lowest parts of the ship, had lain down, and was fast asleep" (Jonah 1:5).

The issue of FIGHTING WITH YOUR YES affects many others unknowingly. Jonah was not even sensitive to what others were going through because of him; but PRIDE and INSENSITIVITY will do that to you every time. The word Insensitivity is defined as [insufficiently aware of other people's feeling and unable to respond to them appropriately; or indifferent to the importance of something and therefore not responding to it].

The prophet was not only insensitive, but also, because of his disobedience, it cost these blue collar businessmen financially. They had to throw their cargo overboard to try to save their lives. All along, Jonah had gotten comfortable in his disobedience and was fast to sleep.

God will use sinners to spiritually wake you up

"So the captain came to him, and said to him, 'What do you mean, sleeper? Arise, call on your God; perhaps your God will consider us, so that we may not perish'" (Jonah 1:6).

First God tells His servant to *"Arise,"* now the non-believer tells him to *"Arise."* If you won't listen to God, will you listen to the voice of a sinner? God is calling you to be a sign to this generation, so I conclude this section with (Isaiah 60:1-3) from the Amplified Bible:

"ARISE [FROM the depression and prostration in which circumstances have kept you; rise to a new life]! Shine—be radiant with the glory of the Lord; for your light is come, and the glory of the Lord is risen upon you! (2) For behold, darkness shall cover the earth, and dense darkness all peoples; but the Lord shall arise upon you, [O Jerusalem], and His glory shall be seen on you. (3) And nations shall come to your light, and kings to the brightness of your rising."

GOD IS JUST WAITING ON YOUR "Y.E.S.!"

Section II Servant Exposed

"And they said to one another, 'Come let us cast lots, that we may know for whose cause this trouble has come upon us.' So they cast lots, and the lot fell on Jonah" **(Jonah 1:7).**

Your calling is always BIGGER than you think

CASTING LOTS had been a method often used to reveal God's purpose in a matter (1 Sam. 14:36-45; 1 Chr. 25:8-31: Acts 1:26).

"The lot is cast into the lap, but the decision is wholly of the Lord—even the events [that seem accidental] are really ordered by Him" (Proverbs 16:33, Amplified).

When a LOT (of PRESSURE) falls on you, how do you handle it? Do you get angry and lash out at others, or do you hide yourself in things such as depression, alcohol, work, bad relationships, etc. In God's eyes, you have an ON PURPOSE LIFE!!! WHY? BECAUSE IT'S HIS PURPOSE AND NOT YOURS!

"Many are the plans in a man's heart, but it is the LORD's purpose that prevails" (Proverbs 19:21, NIV).

Jonah wasn't running from his calling as a prophet of God; he was running from the STRECTHING of his calling as a prophet of God. You must understand that God wants to bless you, but in many cases He must first STRETCH YOU!

Where you've been determines where you are going

"Then they said to Him, 'Please tell us! What is your occupation? And where do you come from? What is your country? And of what people are you" (Jonah 1:8).

The same verse in the NIV Bible says it like this, *"Who is responsible for making all this trouble for us?"* Since this was their occupation these sailors had been in rough seas before, but they understood this storm not to be a normal storm. IT WAS TAILOR MADE BY GOD!

(23) "Those who go down to the sea in ships, who do business on great waters, (24) They see the works of the LORD, and His wonders in the deep. (25) For He commands and raises the stormy wind, which lifts up the waves of the sea" (Psalm 107:23-25).

One of the things the Lord showed me as I was writing this book is that in life we must be careful who we allow in our ship (those who we enter into relationSHIP with). The sailors ask Jonah four questions, and when entering into a relationship (especially marriage) you literally should ask the same questions:

1. What is your occupation? [What do you do for a living: how do you support yourself?]

2. Where do you come from? [What kind of Character & Integrity do you have?]

3. What is your country? [Where was your life shaped: what made you who you are].

4. Of what people are you from? [What is your family like; what's your family history; how do you all get along?]

As you ask questions you also pray to the Lord and ask for WISDOM, KNOWLEDGE, & DISCERNMENT in the process of entering & developing relationships.

Identifying the SOURCE and the SOURCE

"So he said to them, "I am a Hebrew; and I fear the LORD, the God of heaven, who made the sea and the dry land" (Jonah 1:9).

Eventually, in the midst of sinners and the PRESSURE OF SIN you are going to have to CONFESS WHO YOU ARE. Confessions come through words and actions.

"Then the men were exceedingly afraid, and said to him, 'Why have you done this?' For the men knew that he fled from the presence of the LORD, because he had told them" (Jonah 1:10).

Jonah was the SOURCE (the reason the storm occurred), and they now knew that God was the SOURCE (the cause of the storm).

Getting rid of your no for YES

"Then they said to him, 'What shall we do to you that the sea may be calm for us?'—for the sea was growing more tempestuous" (Jonah 1:11).

The Message Bible says it like this, *"What are we going to do with you—to get rid of the storm? By this time the sea was wild, totally out of control."*

Don't ever think that every saved person you come across has to be a part of your life and ministry. When God calls you to do something uniquely assigned to you, not everybody can handle it. There are times that you can have "stormy people" in your life. Misplaced compassion will cause you to think that you have to minister to them, but PLEASE PRAY and ask the Lord, "What should I do with this stormy person in my life?" There are some that God will give you the wisdom & knowledge on how to minister to them, and then there are some that He will tell you to remove from your life.

Again, the Message Bible says in verse 12: *"Jonah said, 'Throw me overboard, into the sea. Then the storm will stop. It's all my fault. I'm the cause of the storm. Get rid of me and you'll get rid of the storm."*

The word OVERBOARD means to discard or get rid of something useless or unwanted. Many times when we are in stormy situations, it's because of stormy people. Rarely will stormy people admit that they are the cause, so you must be determined to get them out of your life.

The storm was so bad that the sailors new (in the natural) that if they threw Jonah overboard that he wouldn't live; but God had already declared that he would LIVE AND NOT DIE! He had an assignment to fulfill!

"So shall My word be that goes forth from My mouth; it shall not return to Me void, but it shall accomplish what I please, and it shall prosper in the thing for which I sent it" (Isaiah 55:11).

Whether God has to work through your NO or around your NO, His WILL shall be FULFILLED; but He is waiting on your Y.E.S.!

Section III The Belly Of Preparation

"Now the LORD had prepared a great fish to swallow Jonah. And Jonah was in the belly of the fish three days and three nights" **(Jonah 1:17).**

THE BELLY OF PREPARATION represents the place of Isolation, Separation, & Sanctification.

ISOLATION

Isolation: [the process or fact of isolating or being isolated]... *"SWALLOWED"*

There are times in our lives (in our service to God) that He has to allow certain situations to swallow us up because many times WE DON'T KNOW HE'S ALL WE NEED UNTIL HE IS ALL WE HAVE! God knows how to DRY UP your resources until you seek Him as your only source (Psalm 63:1-8). The sooner you submit & seek the Lord the sooner God will bring you out.

Jesus said that apart from Him we can do nothing (John 15:5), but as a friend would say to me years ago, "I can show you better than I can tell you!"

SEPARATION

Separation: [the action or state of moving or being moved apart]…*"DIGESTED"*

You will be totally confused if you try to figure God out in the natural because what you see won't make a whole lot of sense. What you thought was REJECTION was actually SEPARATION!

Preparing you for your PURPOSE didn't start the day your purpose showed up (your revelation of it); but it has been in preparation since the day you took your first breath. At the appointed time your purpose INTERSECTS YOUR LIFE!

What road has carried you to this place? Many of us have this in common: we've all been at the same intersection of Life: PAIN LANE & PURPOSE BLVD.! We either run through the stop sign and crash & burn, or we yield to the Spirit of the Lord!

The Apostle Paul's life was going along fine in religion until he had an encounter with Jesus on the road to Damascus (see Acts 9:1-31). Ultimately, he received the revelation that in all that he went through, is going through, and would go through HE WAS SEPARATED FOR THIS!

(15) "But when it pleased God, who separated me from my mother's womb and called me through His grace, (16) to reveal His Son in me, that I might preach Him among the Gentiles, I did not immediately confer with flesh and blood"(Galatians 1:15, 16).

SANCTIFICATION

Sanctification: [to set apart as to declare holy, make legitimate, free from sin; purify, or cause to be acceptable].

In the natural, when something is swallowed (digested) it goes into the belly and is BROKEN-DOWN to be used in the body. Whatever is unusable is considered waste and it is REMOVED from the body. In "The Belly of Preparation" God is removing the waste from His body. You must begin to see that your TIME, TALENT & TREASURES have value when it comes to things concerning the KING-

DOM OF GOD!

"The Belly of Preparation" is also the WOMB of HEALING!

"Before I formed thee in the belly I knew thee; and before thou camest forth out of the womb I sanctified thee, and I ordained thee a prophet to the nations" (Jeremiah 1:5, KJV).

WOMB: [a place of origination and development]

In order for God to PREPARE YOU He must first REPAIR YOU!!! He will fix you, mend you, heal you and put you right. This happens when we see ourselves through the eyes of scripture: *"For he made Him who knew no sin to be sin for us, that we might become the righteousness of God in Him"* (2 Corinthians 5:21). In Christ you have been made RIGHT!

We all have a former life in something, but the scripture says, *"But you were washed, but you were sanctified, but you were justified in the name of the Lord Jesus and by the Spirit of our God"* (1 Corinthians 6:11).

When Jonah sought the Lord in the belly of the fish the bible says, *"So the LORD spoke to the fish, and it vomited*

Jonah onto dry land" (Jonah 2:10).

In this season, God is waiting on His Y.E.S. (Your Expected Submission)! Yes, God knows what it takes to BREAK YOU; but more importantly, He knows what it takes to MAKE YOU!

"No test or temptation that comes your way is beyond the course of what others have had to face. All you need to remember is that God will never let you down; he'll never let you be pushed past your limit; he'll always be there to help you come through it" (1 Corinthians 10:13, The Message Bible).

Section IV Servant Reflection and Freedom

"But I will sacrifice to You with the voice of thanksgiving: I will pay what I have vowed. Salvation is of the LORD" **(Jonah 2:9).**

In the midst of his disobedience and ultimate chastisement from the Lord the prophet Jonah began to seek the Lord. How far down do you have to go until you finally recognize the sovereignty of God; and that God is not going to change the assignment that He has given you?

Let's look at the prayer of Jonah in two parts:

The servant acknowledges God's Sovereignty

God's Sovereignty means [God's supreme authority]. Sovereignty means that God, as the ruler of the Universe, has the right to do whatever He wants. He is in complete control of everything that happens (see Psalm 115:3; Isaiah 46:10; Daniel 4:35; Romans 9:20). The Bible says that Jonah finally *"prayed to the LORD his God from the fish's belly"* (Jonah 2:1).

(2) "I cried out to the LORD because of my affliction, and He answered me. Out of the belly of Sheol I cried, and you heard my voice. For you cast me into the deep, into the heart of the seas, and the floods surrounded me; All Your billows and Your waves passed over me."

When was the last time you cried out to God? He cried out because of his *"affliction!"* An AFFLICTION is [a condition of great physical or mental distress]. When our confidence is in Him even in our afflictions we know that He hears and answers us.

Jonah compares the belly of the fish to *"Sheol"* which is translated as the grave, hell, or the pit (a low place). The low place is also a place of DEPRESSION, which is defined as [a psychiatric disorder showing symptoms such as persistent feelings of hopelessness, dejection, poor concentration, lack of energy, inability to sleep, and sometimes suicidal tendencies]. I do want you to understand that if you experience any of these symptoms, it can be caused by depression or possibly several other factors. The bottom-line is that no matter how you got there you are in a LOW PLACE but God can BRING YOU OUT!

Are You Still Fighting With Your Y.E.S.

Many times God has to isolate you before He can elevate you. He will use our disobedience as a tool of repositioning. Unfortunately, God has to allow things to come upon us in this life in which our money can't buy us out; family can't bail us out; and your mind can't work it out. But no matter how far you get from God in your disobedience when you turn back to God in repentance YOU WILL HEAR HIM AGAIN!

"O LORD, you have searched me and you know me. (2) You know when I sit and when I rise; you perceive my thoughts from afar. (3) You discern my going out and my lying down; you are familiar with all my ways. (4) Before a word is on my tongue you know it completely, O LORD" (Psalm 139:1-4, NIV).

God is familiar with all of our ways and He knows exactly what you need, and how much you need to bring you back to the place of obedience. Disobedience puts you in BONDAGE but no matter how far down you go, your CRYING OUT can BRING YOU OUT!!!

(13) "Then they cried out to the LORD in their trouble, and He saved them out of their distresses. (14) He brought them out of darkness and the shadow of death, and broke

their chains in pieces" (Psalm 107:13, 14).

The servant submits to God's Sovereignty

(4) "I said, 'I have been banished from your sight; yet I will look again toward your holy temple (5) The engulfing waters threatened me, the deep surrounded me; seaweed was wrapped around my head. (6) To the roots of the mountains I sank down; the earth beneath barred me in forever. But you brought my life up from the pit, O LORD my God. (7) When my life was ebbing away, I remembered you, LORD, and my prayer rose to you, to your holy temple. (8) Those who cling to worthless idols forfeit the grace that could be theirs. (9) But I, with a song of thanksgiving, will sacrifice to you. What I have vowed I will make good. Salvation comes from the LORD." (Jonah 2:4-9)

Many times we look for a word from God, but we have not received it because of our WRONG POSITION. In order to move out of that place you must do something called humbling yourself.

(6) "He gives more grace. Therefore He says: God resists the proud, but gives grace to the humble. (7) Therefore submit to God. Resist the devil and he will flee from you. (10) Humble yourselves in the sight of the Lord, and

He will lift you up" (James 4:6, 7, 10).

Your wrong POSITION should lead to your SUBMISSION, which will bring you back to your MISSION. Jonah understood as we should also that God was not trying to destroy him; He actually wanted to RESTORE him. Many times, what we are going through can be extended if that is your total focus. I believe that's what King David understood when he said, *"I will bless the LORD at all times; His praise shall continually be in my mouth. (2) My soul shall make its boast in the LORD; the humble shall hear of it and be glad. (3) Oh, magnify the LORD with me, and let us exalt His name together. (4) I sought the LORD, and He heard me, and delivered me from all my fears"* (Psalm 34:1-4).

WHATEVER YOU STRUGGLE WITH

GOD STANDS READY TO DELIVER YOU!

As servants of God, we must understand that extreme CORRECTION is not REJECTION, it's for our DIRECTION. One of the greatest tests in your relationship with God concerning your maturity is can you declare your FREEDOM while you are still IN THE BELLY of PREPARATION? Everything that you depended on (the *"worthless idols"*) must be cast down and removed in order for you to see the TRUE & LIVING GOD! Jonah 4:8 in the Amplified says, *"Those who pay regard to false, useless and worthless idols forsake their own [Source of] mercy and lovingkindness."*

The Lord makes it clear in His word: *(2) "I am the LORD your God, who brought you out of the land of Egypt, out of the house of bondage. (3) You shall have no other gods before Me. (4) You shall not make for yourself a carved image—any likeness of anything that is in heaven above, or that is in the earth beneath, or that is in the water under the earth; (5) you shall not bow down to them nor serve them. For I, the LORD your God, am a jealous God"* (Exodus 20:2-5). God is not only jealous, but the scripture also declares His *"name is Jealous"* (Exodus 34:14). Have you ever made a sacrifice for someone and gave up all that you had because they came to you in desperate need. Then you found out that what you made a sacrifice for, they gave away freely without regard to your sacrifice. If you can understand that then you can understand our God being Jealous for YOU! He gave us all that He had in our Lord & Savior Jesus Christ (John 3:16)!

Section V The Lord Speaks/The Servant Hears

"So the LORD spoke to the fish, and it vomited Jonah onto dry land" (Jonah 2:10).

When God Speaks

Whatever God speak has to come to pass!

(8) "For My thoughts are not your thoughts, nor are your ways My ways, says the LORD. (9) For as the heavens are higher than the earth, so are My ways higher than your ways, and My thoughts than your thoughts. (10) For as the rain comes down, and the snow from heaven, and do not return there, but water the earth, and make it bring forth and bud, that it may give seed to the sower and bread to the eater, (11) So shall My word be that goes forth from My mouth; It shall not return to Me void, but it shall accomplish what I please, And it shall proper in the thing for which I sent it" (Isaiah 55:8-11).

When your issue is with God, and your obedience to Him, it takes God to speak to your fish (your situation or circumstance). The NIV says, *"the Lord commanded the fish."* The Lord can not only speak to your situation, but He can also speak to you in your situation.

Lazarus had a situation called death, but Jesus spoke to him in the midst of his situation: *"Lazarus, come forth!"* (John 11:43). Just as the Lord speaks to others circumstances & situations, or speaks to others in the midst of them, He can do it for you too if you TRUST HIM!

The role of the enemy

Because your spiritual enemies (demons & devils) can play a role in all that you are going through (because of past open doors in your life), there are many times that they are not willing to let you go. But when God speaks to your situation it must be obedient to "vomit" you out! Something that is vomited is something that is removed (expelled or ejected) by force.

"The kingdom of heaven has been forcefully advancing, and forceful men lay hold of it" (Matthew 11:12, NIV).

Many times as I mentioned before when we are going through, we are looking to hear a word from the Lord. Because of your Y.E.S. (Your Expected Submission) God can and will speak to your situation!

Ears to Hear

(1) "Now the word of the LORD came to Jonah the second time, saying, (2) Arise, go to Nineveh, that great city, and preach to it the message that I tell you" (Jonah 3:1, 2).

Your Y.E.S. will cause you to gain your hearing (spiritual sensitivity) back.

(23) "If any man has ears to hear, let him be listening, and perceive and comprehend. (24) And He said to them, Be careful what you are hearing. The measure [of thought and study] you give [to the truth you hear] will be the measure [of virtue and knowledge] that comes back to you, and more [besides] will be given to you who hear" (Mark 4:23, 24, Amp.)

The People are Waiting

(35) "Then Jesus went about all the cities and villages, teaching in their synagogues, preaching the gospel of

the kingdom, and healing every sickness and every disease among the people. (36) But when He saw the multitudes, He was moved with compassion for them, because they were weary and scattered, like sheep having no shepherd. (37) Then He said to His disciples, 'The harvest truly is plentiful, but the laborers are few. (38) Therefore pray the Lord of the harvest to send out laborers into His harvest'" (Matthew 9:35-38).

Jesus told His disciples to pray for laborers to be sent out into the harvest. Many times as you pray that prayer you can not only be praying for other laborers, but you can also be praying for yourself (your own labor).

There are many people who can't come out of sin and bondage until Y.E.S. (Your Expected Submission)! After ALL that you've been through (fighting Y.E.S.), it's time for you to ARISE and go in obedience to fulfill the will of God in and for your life.

When Jonah was obedient to God and preached to Nineveh the results were that *"the people of Nineveh believed God, proclaimed a fast, and put on sackcloth, from the greatest to the least of them"* (Jonah 3:5). The king of Nineveh received the word and repented and caused the nation to do the same. *"God saw their works, that they turned from their evil way; and God relented from the disaster that He had said He would bring upon them, and He did not do it"* (Jonah 3:10).

The result of Jonah's obedience was the obedience of those who heard the truth of God's word through Him. Hallelujah!

God is Not Through With You Yet

Unfortunately, at the end of the story God still had to deal with the attitude of His servant Jonah, because although he did the work he was upset about the results: *"It displeased Jonah exceedingly, and he became angry"* (Jonah 4:1). Why was Jonah so angry? He was angry because God had mercy on someone he didn't like! That also says that even though he did the work there were still areas of unforgiveness in his life that still needed to be dealt with. The Lord also asked Jonah, *"Is it right for you to be angry?"* (Jonah 4:4)

You must remember that the work is the Lord's and NOT YOURS! He says in His word, *"I will have mercy on whom I will have mercy, and I will have compassion on whom I will have compassion"* (Exodus 33:19, NIV).

One of the key ingredients in deliverance ministry is to always know that as God has you working on His behalf He is also continually working on you, and on your behalf! This means that we should always have times of SELF-EXAMINATION, as well as asking the Lord to continually SEARCH US.

(5) "Examine and test and evaluate your own selves, to see whether you are holding to your faith and showing the proper fruits of it. Test and prove yourselves, [not Christ]. Do you not yourselves realize and know (thoroughly by and ever-increasing experience) that Jesus Christ is in you? (6) But I hope you will recognize and know that we are not disapproved on trial and rejected! (2 Corinthians 13:5, 6, Amp.)

Since all of us operate in some form of pride one of the best ways to break it is to continually *"Examine test and evaluate your own selves, to see whether you are holding to your faith and showing the proper fruits of it."* This very thing is what makes us acceptable to God and allows Him to work through us. From this we are known by our fruits, which are seen by the world. Since we have the Spirit of Christ in us, we know whether our actions are pleasing or unpleasing to the Lord by the grief we feel in our spirit. In the Message Bible it says, *"Don't grieve God. Don't break his heart. His Holy Spirit, moving and breathing in you, is the most intimate part of your life, making you fit for himself. Don't take such a gift for granted. Make a clean break with all cutting, backbiting, profane talk. Be gentle with one another, sensitive. Forgive one another as quickly and thoroughly as God in Christ forgave you"* (Eph. 4:30-32, TMB)

It's impossible to say that you serve God without having the desire to serve God's people (no matter how bad they are). The Lord has been waiting on you to get into the proper place so that He can show Himself strong through you: *"For the eyes of the LORD run to and fro throughout the whole earth, to show Himself strong on behalf of those whose heart is loyal to Him"* (2 Chr. 16:9).

Although the Lord already knows you, you must continually humble yourself and open up yourself to be searched:

(23) "Search me [thoroughly], O God, and know my heart! Try me, and know my thoughts! (24) And see if there is any wicked or hurtful way in me, and lead me in the way everlasting" (Psalm 139:23, 24, Amp.)

As you continually examine yourself and ask the Lord to search you that gives the enemy no room to operate in your life. The example we have is when Jesus was coming to the end of His earthly work and ministry, He said, *"the ruler of this world is coming, and he has nothing in Me"* (John 14:30). In the same way, when the enemy comes (he will come), we must make sure that there is nothing in us that he can work with. Our life (now belonging to Him) must be a life that lines up with the cross because, *"those who are Christ's have crucified the flesh with its passions and desires"* (Gal. 5:24)

Conclusion

As you fulfilled the call of God on your life, it has the ability to break spiritual bondages and set families, churches, neighborhoods, communities, cities, states, countries, and ultimately entire nations FREE!!!

YOU HAVE THE POWER IN YOU!

"But you shall receive power—ability, efficiency and might—when the Holy Spirit has come upon you; and you shall be My witnesses in Jerusalem and all Judea and Samaria and to the ends—the very bounds—of the earth" (Acts 1:8, Amp.).

LET TODAY BE THE DAY OF **Y.E.S.**

(Your Expected Submission)!!!

Please repeat the following prayer and know that today I touch and agree with you in thanking God for your **Y.E.S.!**

Heavenly Father,

I repent of my sins, and I ask that you would forgive me of my disobedience & rebellion against any assignment that you have given me that I refused to do because of my carnal attitude toward the people and or situations.

I declare YES to You and asked that you would empower me from on high to fulfill my assignment so that hearts would be changed, people would be healed, demons would be cast out, darkness would be lifted, and people would be delivered from the bondages of sin. I thank you for your grace and mercy in my life that I now extend to those who You have already extended it to.

Today I release pride, judgment, condemnation, anger, hatred, bitterness, resentment, unforgiveness, and any other negative emotion that has hindered me from the work you have called me to do. I forgive those who have hurt me, just as you have forgiven me. I ask that you would continue to reveal yourself in me so that the fruits of my labor would be seen and that you would be glorified. In Jesus name… Amen!

MAY GOD CONTINUE TO BLESS YOUR WORK & MINISTRY

About The Author

PASTOR THOMAS C. MARBURY is the Senior Pastor of Kingdom Apostolic Church International (K.A.C.I.).

Pastor Marbury's main focus in ministry is renewing the mind of believers so that they can be all that God has called them to be. He is a pastor's pastor, teacher, conference speaker, biblical counselor, spiritual father, and author.

Pastor Marbury is also an Apostolically SENT Pastor who believes that TRUE MINISTRY work is not limited to the four walls of the church. He is overseer of LOGOS MEN'S FELLOWSHIP which is a group of kingdom minded men from different church's and ministries with a common goal of restoring and building up men for the kingdom work God has called them to do. Then sending them home as better fathers, husbands, brothers, sons, etc. The theme of the ministry is "Reaching out to Men and Reaching up to God."

Connect With Thomas Online

www.ThomasCMarbury.com

www.facebook.com/ThomasCMarbury

www.twitter.com/ThomasCMarbury

www.instagram.com/ThomasCMarbury

www.ingramcontent.com/pod-product-compliance
Lightning Source LLC
Chambersburg PA
CBHW021137300426
44113CB00006B/462